Ruth
Loyal & Blessed

A Bible Study on the Book of Ruth

Compiled by Joani Ross
#revivormation
© 2016

#Revivormation

We are praying for a REVIVORMATION,

a new word for a new movement.

A new awakening.

Reformation (from Latin reformatio, lit. "restoration, renewal") + Revival... a spiritual reawakening from a state of dormancy or stagnation in the life of a believer. It encompasses the resurfacing of a love for God, an appreciation of God's holiness, a passion for His Word and His church, a convicting awareness of personal and corporate sin, a spirit of humility, and a desire for repentance and growth in righteousness. Revival invigorates and sometimes deepens a believer's faith, opening his or her eyes to the truth in a fresh, new way. It generally involves the connotation of a fresh start with a clean slate, marking a new beginning of a life lived in obedience to God. Revival breaks the charm and power of the world, which blinds the eyes of men, and generates both the will and power to live in the world but not of the world.*

*Revival definition from gotquestions.org

Welcome

Welcome to our study on the fascinating book of Ruth. Our prayer is that you love to study God's word and that through this study you learn more about who God is and how he works in our lives.

We will meet and learn about an ordinary, but amazing, woman. She had a tragic turn in her life, but God used it for good.

Join us to learn how under God's powerful provision and plan, a poor widow in a foreign land – through loyalty, hard work and living in God's will – becomes the great grandmother of Kind David.

Our memory verse for this study is Romans 8:28...

AND WE KNOW THAT IN ALL THINGS **GOD** WORKS FOR THE GOOD OF THOSE WHO LOVE HIM WHO HAVE BEEN **CALLED** ACCORDING TO HIS PURPOSE

ROMANS 8:28

Contents

Week 1: Ruth Chapter 1
   Tragedy & Loyalty

Week 2: Ruth Chapter 2
   Harvesting

Week 3: Ruth Chapter 3
   Ruth Visits Boaz

Week 4: Ruth Chapter 4
   The Redeemer, Our Redeemer

Attachments: Ice Breaker Questions & Service Ideas

Week 1: Tragedy & Loyalty

Warm Up with tea and treats
- Draw an image or some key words of what loyalty means to you

Introductions & Name Game
- Go around the room and introduce yourself (name, age, something about you, & one word that describes you using the first letter of your name...Artistic Anabelle).
- As each new person introduces themselves they say the previous girls' names and one word descriptor.
- At the end take a volunteer to go around and repeat everyone's names.

Why Bible Study
- Take volunteers to say why they wanted to do this Bible study and what they hope to get out of it.

Review Bible Study Format
- One chapter a week for four weeks.
- Discussions during Bible study with homework during the week.
- Discuss service project & items needed (see back of guide for ideas)

Open in Prayer to start the study

Read Ruth Chapter 1
- Listed on the following pages 2-4.

A Family Tragedy: Famine and Death

1 During the time of the judges there was a famine in the land of Judah. So a man from Bethlehem in Judah went to live as a resident foreigner in the region of Moab, along with his wife and two sons. ² (Now the man's name was Elimelech, his wife was Naomi, and his two sons were Mahlon and Kilion. They were of the clan of Ephrath from Bethlehem in Judah.) They entered the region of Moab and settled there. ³ Sometime later Naomi's husband Elimelech died, so she and her two sons were left alone. ⁴ So her sons married Moabite women. (One was named Orpah and the other Ruth.) And they continued to live there about ten years. ⁵ Then Naomi's two sons, Mahlon and Kilion, also died. So the woman was left all alone—bereaved of her two children as well as her husband! ⁶ So she decided to return home from the region of Moab, accompanied by her daughters-in-law, because while she was living in Moab she had heard that the Lord had shown concern for his people, reversing the famine by providing abundant crops.

Ruth Returns with Naomi

⁷ Now as she and her two daughters-in-law began to leave the place where she had been living to return to the land of Judah, ⁸ Naomi said to her two daughters-in-law, "Listen to me! Each of you should return to your mother's home! May the Lord show you the same kind of devotion that you have shown to your deceased husbands and to me! ⁹ May the Lord enable each of you to find security in the home of a new husband!" Then she kissed them goodbye and they wept loudly. ¹⁰ But they said to her, "No! We will return with you to your people."

¹¹ But Naomi replied, "Go back home, my daughters! There is no reason for you to return to Judah with me! I am no longer capable of giving birth to sons who might become your husbands! ¹² Go back home, my daughters! For I am too old to get married again. Even if I thought that there was hope that I could get married tonight and conceive sons, ¹³ surely you would not want to wait until they were old enough to marry! Surely you would not remain unmarried all that time! No, my daughters, you must not return with me. For my intense suffering is too much for you to bear. For the LORD is afflicting me!"

¹⁴ Again they wept loudly. Then Orpah kissed her mother-in-law goodbye, but Ruth clung tightly to her. ¹⁵ So Naomi said, "Look, your sister-in-law is returning to her people and to her god. Follow your sister-in-law back home!" ¹⁶ But Ruth replied,

"Stop urging me to abandon you! For wherever you go, I will go. Wherever you live, I will live. Your people will become my people, and your God will become my God. ¹⁷ Wherever you die, I will die—and there I will be buried. May the LORD punish me severely if I do not keep my promise! Only death will be able to separate me from you!"

¹⁸ When Naomi realized that Ruth was determined to go with her, she stopped trying to dissuade her. ¹⁹ So the two of them journeyed together until they arrived in Bethlehem.

Naomi and Ruth Arrive in Bethlehem

When they entered Bethlehem, the whole village was excited about their arrival. The women of the village said, "Can this be Naomi?" [20] But she replied to them, "Don't call me 'Naomi'! Call me 'Mara' because the Sovereign One has treated me very harshly. [21] I left here full, but the LORD has caused me to return empty-handed. Why do you call me 'Naomi,' seeing that the LORD has opposed me, and the Sovereign One has caused me to suffer?" [22] So Naomi returned, accompanied by her Moabite daughter-in-law Ruth, who came back with her from the region of Moab. (Now they arrived in Bethlehem at the beginning of the barley harvest.)

When did this story take place? (v.1)
- During the time of _____.

When the Jewish people were freed by God from slavery in Egypt, they didn't have a king or ruler like the other countries. God was their king. Instead they had Judges that tried to unify the people, get them to repent, deal with spiritual issues of the time. They were sometimes military leaders who also dealt with physical threats to the Jewish people.

Why was Naomi's family in Moab? (v.1)

When God was guiding the Israelites out of Egypt through the wilderness to the Promised Land (Canaan), he promised them if they were obedient, and serve no other gods but Him, he would take care of them and they would have plenty of crops with no fear of famine.

What does it suggest that families had to leave Israel because of a famine?

What happened that caused Naomi to want to leave their home in Moab? (v. 3-5)

How was Ruth related to Naomi? Was Ruth a fellow Israelite? (v. 4)

Ruth was a Moabite. She wasn't a Jew and she didn't grow up with our God as her God. The Moabites has a scandalous past and a turbulent history. After the destruction of Sodom and Gomorrah (places of evil), Abraham's nephew Lot had children with his daughters that became the ancestors of the Moabites and Ammonites. They did evil things and worshiped false gods.

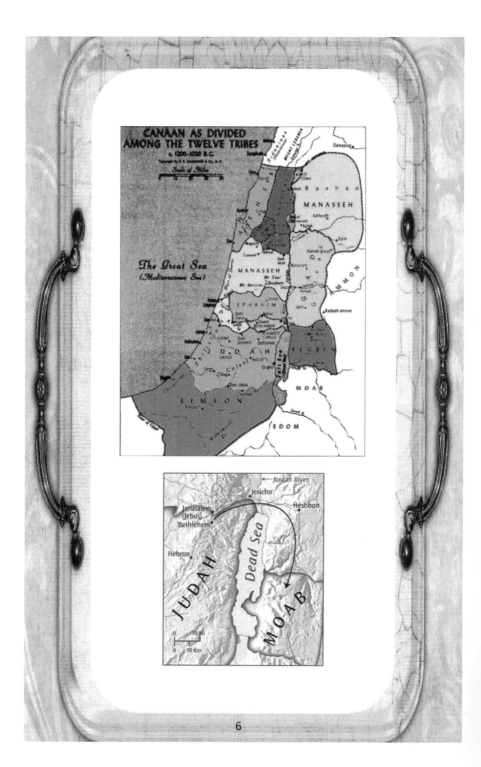

Back to Bethlehem

What does Naomi say to her daughter-in-laws (Ruth and Orpah) as they are heading out of Moab to Judah? (v. 7-10)

What is the response of both girls? (v. 10)

But Naomi insists and tries to convince them again to go back to their homes. How would you describe Naomi's state of mind as she tries to convince them not to leave with her in v. 11-13?

Why do you think Naomi changed her mind and wanted to talk them into staying?

There was not a good relationship between the Moabites and the Israelites.

When Naomi mentions not having sons for them to marry, she is referring to a custom back then of providing for childless widows by giving them a husband from among the dead husband's brothers. But Naomi had no more sons to give them as a husband. She had lost her entire family.

What is Ruth's final reply to Naomi in v. 16-17?

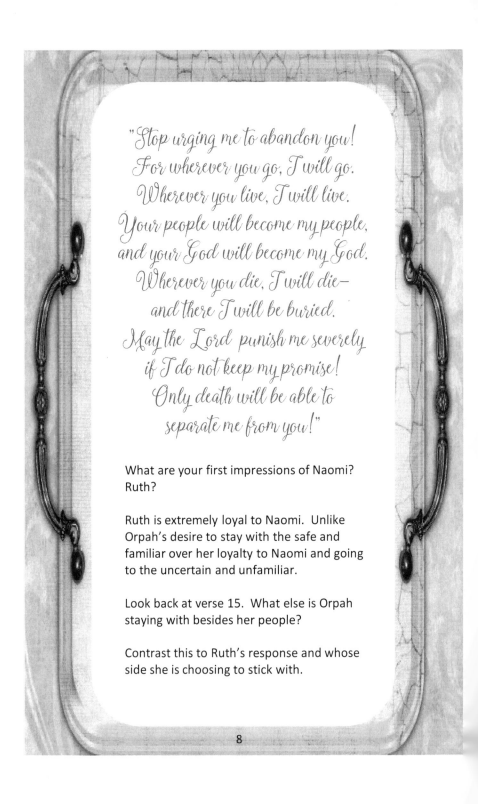

> "Stop urging me to abandon you!
> For wherever you go, I will go.
> Wherever you live, I will live.
> Your people will become my people,
> and your God will become my God.
> Wherever you die, I will die—
> and there I will be buried.
> May the Lord punish me severely
> if I do not keep my promise!
> Only death will be able to
> separate me from you!"

What are your first impressions of Naomi? Ruth?

Ruth is extremely loyal to Naomi. Unlike Orpah's desire to stay with the safe and familiar over her loyalty to Naomi and going to the uncertain and unfamiliar.

Look back at verse 15. What else is Orpah staying with besides her people?

Contrast this to Ruth's response and whose side she is choosing to stick with.

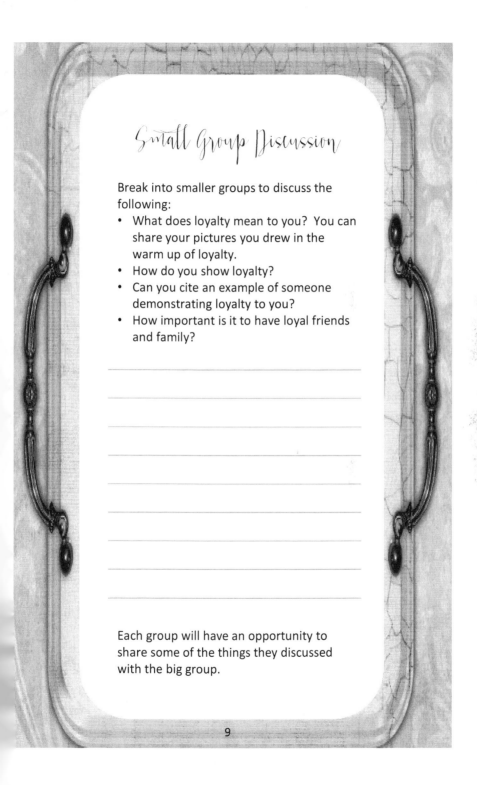

Small Group Discussion

Break into smaller groups to discuss the following:
- What does loyalty mean to you? You can share your pictures you drew in the warm up of loyalty.
- How do you show loyalty?
- Can you cite an example of someone demonstrating loyalty to you?
- How important is it to have loyal friends and family?

Each group will have an opportunity to share some of the things they discussed with the big group.

What can you say about Naomi's state of mind as she enters Bethlehem? What does she say they should call her and what does it mean? (v. 20-22)

Has Naomi really returned empty handed as she states in v. 21?

Do you think God causes suffering?

Suffering is a consequence of evil. God is not the author of evil. He wants what is best for us and he is good. But he has given us free will and we can use the gifts we have been given for good or evil. Sin in the world and sinful decisions can bring suffering to even the innocent and righteous people.

Based on what we have seen about Ruth so far, what makes her an unlikely Bible hero?
- She is not an Israelite.
- She is a descendant of ancestors born from sinful behavior and pagan people.
- She is a foreigner, poor and widowed.
- She is from a people who were traditional enemies of Israel.

But God's ways are not our ways!

"And we know that in all things God works for the good of those who love him, who have been called according to his purpose."
Romans 8:28

Week 1 Homework

- Reread Ruth chapter 1 and the things we discussed about the chapter.
- Think more about loyalty. What it means to be loyal and how you can be a loyal friend.
- Think about what loyalties are important to you as a Christian. What do you think the cost of these loyalties might be?
- Think about one service project you can do during the course of this 4 week study.
- Memorize Romans 8:28.

"We know that in all things God works for the good of those who love Him and have been called according to His purpose."
Romans 8:28

* If you are interested in ordering a keepsake necklace for the study, you can visit the fabulous Shakespeare's Sisters Boutique at http://www.etsy.com/shop/ShakespearesSisters

Week 2: Harvesting

Warm Up with tea and treats
- Write some thoughts about hard word

Memory Verse
- Take volunteers to recite the memory verse and get their prize.

Question Box
- Have the girls take turns answering a questions from the box (sample questions in the back of the guide).

Open in Prayer to start the study

Recap of Week 1
- Pick a volunteer to review week 1 discussion
- Review homework
- Discuss service project ideas

Read Ruth Chapter 2
- Listed on the following pages 13-15.

Ruth Works in the Field of Boaz

2:1 Now Naomi had a relative on her husband's side of the family named Boaz. He was a wealthy, prominent man from the clan of Elimelech. [2] One day Ruth the Moabite said to Naomi, "Let me go to the fields so I can gather grain behind whoever permits me to do so." Naomi replied, "You may go, my daughter." [3] So Ruth went and gathered grain in the fields behind the harvesters. Now she just happened to end up in the portion of the field belonging to Boaz, who was from the clan of Elimelech.

Boaz and Ruth Meet

[4] Now at that very moment, Boaz arrived from Bethlehem and greeted the harvesters, "May the Lord be with you!" They replied, "May the Lord bless you!" [5] Boaz asked his servant in charge of the harvesters, "To whom does this young woman belong?" [6] The servant in charge of the harvesters replied, "She's the young Moabite woman who came back with Naomi from the region of Moab. [7] She asked, 'May I follow the harvesters and gather grain among the bundles?' Since she arrived she has been working hard from this morning until now—except for sitting in the resting hut a short time."

[8] So Boaz said to Ruth, "Listen carefully, my dear! Do not leave to gather grain in another field. You need not go beyond the limits of this field. You may go along beside my female workers. [9] Take note of the field where the men are harvesting and follow behind with the female workers. I will tell the men to leave you alone. When you are thirsty, you may go to the water jars and drink some of the water the servants draw."

¹⁰ Ruth knelt before him with her forehead to the ground and said to him, "Why are you so kind and so attentive to me, even though I am a foreigner?" ¹¹ Boaz replied to her, "I have been given a full report of all that you have done for your mother-in-law following the death of your husband—how you left your father and your mother, as well as your homeland, and came to live among people you did not know previously. ¹² May the LORD reward your efforts! May your acts of kindness be repaid fully by the LORD God of Israel, from whom you have sought protection!" ¹³ She said, "You really are being kind to me, sir, for you have reassured and encouraged me, your servant, even though I am not one of your servants!"

¹⁴ Later during the mealtime Boaz said to her, "Come here and have some food! Dip your bread in the vinegar!" So she sat down beside the harvesters. Then he handed her some roasted grain. She ate until she was full and saved the rest. ¹⁵ When she got up to gather grain, Boaz told his male servants, "Let her gather grain even among the bundles! Don't chase her off! ¹⁶ Make sure you pull out ears of grain for her and drop them so she can gather them up. Don't tell her not to!" ¹⁷ So she gathered grain in the field until evening. When she threshed what she had gathered, it came to about thirty pounds of barley!

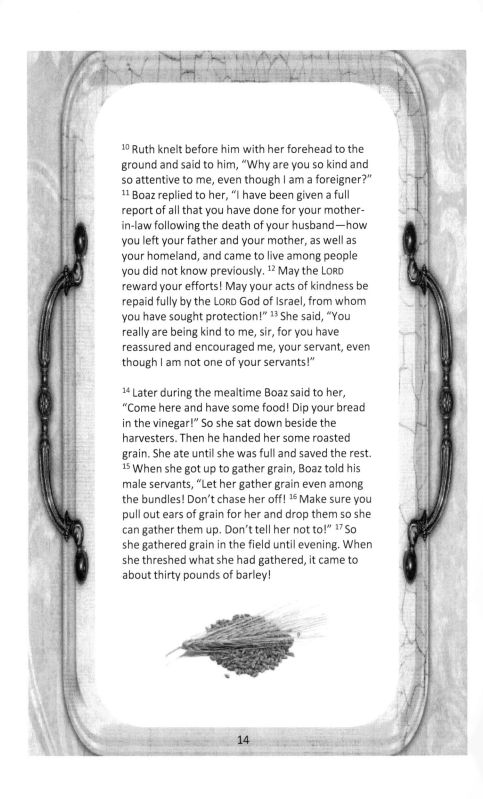

Ruth Returns to Naomi

[18] She carried it back to town, and her mother-in-law saw how much grain she had gathered. Then Ruth gave her the roasted grain she had saved from mealtime. [19] Her mother-in-law asked her, "Where did you gather grain today? Where did you work? May the one who took notice of you be rewarded!" So Ruth told her mother-in-law with whom she had worked. She said, "The name of the man with whom I worked today is Boaz." [20] Naomi said to her daughter-in-law, "May he be rewarded by the Lord because he has shown loyalty to the living on behalf of the dead!" Then Naomi said to her, "This man is a close relative of ours; he is our guardian." [21] Ruth the Moabite replied, "He even told me, 'You may go along beside my servants until they have finished gathering all my harvest!'" [22] Naomi then said to her daughter-in-law Ruth, "It is good, my daughter, that you should go out to work with his female servants. That way you will not be harmed, which could happen in another field." [23] So Ruth worked beside Boaz's female servants, gathering grain until the end of the barley harvest as well as the wheat harvest. After that she stayed home with her mother-in-law.

Ruth works in the fields

What does Ruth do once in Bethlehem? (v. 2-3)

What does this say about Ruth's character?

Read Leviticus 19:9-10
> "'When you gather in the harvest of your land, you must not completely harvest the corner of your field, and you must not gather up the gleanings of your harvest. You must not pick your vineyard bare, and you must not gather up the fallen grapes of your vineyard. You must leave them for the poor and the foreigner. I am the LORD your God."

How are we seeing this play out with Ruth?

What does this say about how God wants to take care of the less fortunate?

Whose field did Ruth "just happen" to be working in? (v.3)

What did verse 1 tell us about Boaz?

Boaz and Ruth Meet

What report did the foreman give to Boaz about Ruth when asked? V. 6-7)

What instructions does Boaz give Ruth? (v. 8-9)

How does Ruth respond in return? (v. 10)

How does Boaz respond in v. 11-12 & 14-16?

How does Naomi describe Boaz to Ruth in v. 20?

In some other versions the word 'guardian' is translated as 'guardian-redeemer'. This is someone who has the authority to exercise the right of redemption over Naomi and her kin under the covenant laws. There were three qualifications to be fulfilled under the law:
- He must be related by blood to those he redeems
- He must have the necessary resources to pay the price of redemption
- He must be willing to redeem

Small Group Discussion

Break into smaller groups to discuss the following:
- Put yourself in Ruth's place. How would it feel to be a foreigner, needing to work hard to support your mother-in-law?
- When times are rough and you are feeling at your lowest, do you tend to feel sorry for yourself and stay put or do you take action to do something about it?
- What example does Ruth give us about how to respond in difficult situations?
- Do you think it was "by chance" that Ruth was in Boaz's field or do you think God had something to do with it?

_____
_____
_____
_____
_____

Each group will have an opportunity to share some of the things they discussed with the big group.

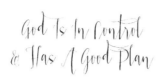
God Is In Control & Has A Good Plan

Look back over the words you wrote about hard work before our study began. Do you feel the same way after our discussions today?

Think about the several examples we have seen so far of God working in the life of Ruth:
- Ruth unknowingly chose a field belonging to Naomi's kinsman
- Boaz just happens to visit his workers the day Ruth is working
- Boaz just happens to notice Ruth among all the workers

Do you really believe that God is in control and works all things for good, as we are memorizing in our verse for the study?

"And we know that in all things God works for the good of those who love him, who have been called according to his purpose."
Romans 8:28

What keeps you from being able to believe this statement?

Week 2 Homework

- Reread Ruth chapter 2 and the things we discussed about the chapter.
- Think more about your response when things aren't going your way.
- Think more about your belief and confidence in our memory verse – that God can work all things for the good of those who love him, who have been called according to his purposes. Think about what it means to be called according to his purposes.
- Think more about your service project.
- Start collecting items for our group service project during our last session together.
- Memorize Romans 8:28.

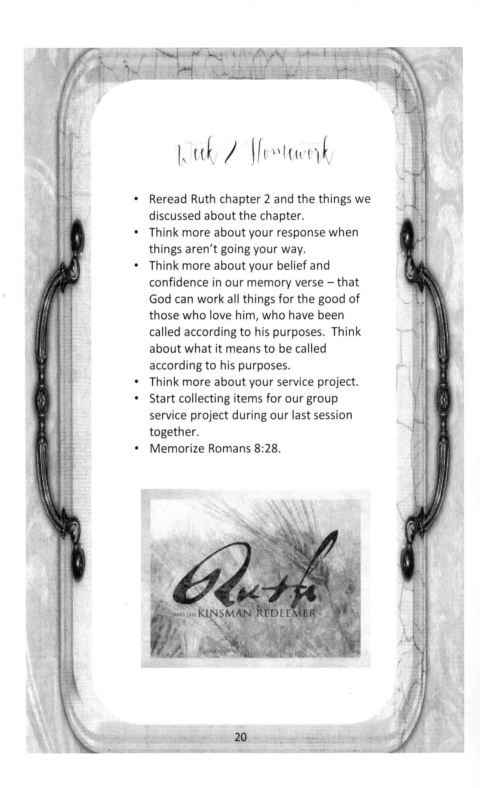

Week 3: Ruth Visits Boaz

Warm Up with tea and treats
- Make a list of the things you think would describe the traits of someone with good character.
- Write on an index card something interesting about you that other people wouldn't know. Don't include your name.

Memory Verse
- Take volunteers to recite the memory verse and get their prize.

Guess Who
- Read the interesting facts from the girls on the index cards. The group guesses who the card belongs to.

Open in Prayer to start the study

Recap of Week 2
- Pick a volunteer to review week 2 discussion
- Review homework
- Discuss service project ideas

Read Ruth Chapter 3
- Listed on the following pages 22-23

Naomi Instructs Ruth

3:1 At that time, Naomi, her mother-in-law, said to her, "My daughter, I must find a home for you so you will be secure. ² Now Boaz, with whose female servants you worked, is our close relative. Look, tonight he is winnowing barley at the threshing floor. ³ So bathe yourself, rub on some perfumed oil, and get dressed up. Then go down to the threshing floor. But don't let the man know you're there until he finishes his meal. ⁴ When he gets ready to go to sleep, take careful notice of the place where he lies down. Then go, uncover his legs, and lie down beside him. He will tell you what you should do." ⁵ Ruth replied to Naomi, "I will do everything you have told me to do."

Ruth Visits Boaz

⁶ So she went down to the threshing floor and did everything her mother-in-law had instructed her to do. ⁷ When Boaz had finished his meal and was feeling satisfied, he lay down to sleep at the far end of the grain heap. Then Ruth crept up quietly, uncovered his legs, and lay down beside him. ⁸ In the middle of the night he was startled and turned over. Now he saw a woman lying beside him! ⁹ He said, "Who are you?" She replied, "I am Ruth, your servant. Marry your servant, for you are a guardian of the family interests." ¹⁰ He said, "May you be rewarded by the Lord, my dear! This act of devotion is greater than what you did before. For you have not sought to marry one of the young men, whether rich or poor.

¹¹ Now, my dear, don't worry! I intend to do for you everything you propose, for everyone in the village knows that you are a worthy woman. ¹² Now yes, it is true that I am a guardian, but there is another guardian who is a closer relative than I am. ¹³ Remain here tonight. Then in the morning, if he agrees to marry you, fine, let him do so. But if he does not want to do so, I promise, as surely as the LORD lives, to marry you. Sleep here until morning." ¹⁴ So she slept beside him until morning. She woke up while it was still dark. Boaz thought, "No one must know that a woman visited the threshing floor." ¹⁵ Then he said, "Hold out the shawl you are wearing and grip it tightly." As she held it tightly, he measured out about sixty pounds of barley into the shawl and put it on her shoulders. Then he went into town, ¹⁶ and she returned to her mother-in-law.

Ruth Returns to Naomi

When Ruth returned to her mother-in-law, Naomi asked, "How did things turn out for you, my daughter?" Ruth told her about all the man had done for her. ¹⁷ She said, "He gave me these sixty pounds of barley, for he said to me, 'Do not go to your mother-in-law empty-handed.'" ¹⁸ Then Naomi said, "Stay put, my daughter, until you know how the matter turns out. For the man will not rest until he has taken care of the matter today."

Naomi's Instructions

What instructions does Naomi give Ruth in v. 1-4?

According to the teaching of Jewish rabbis, Ruth's preparations were symbolic of her conversion:
- First she washed herself, purifying herself from her earlier paganism (believing in false gods in Moab)
- In anointing herself, she accepted her covenant obligations in the Jewish law
- In dressing she put on her Sabbath garments in full observance of the Jewish law.

In Jewish times, the uncovering was symbolic of asking Boaz to be her kinsmen redeemer and to marry her.

What do you think about Naomi's suggestions about Boaz not knowing who it was that was in there with him?

Do you think Naomi was suggesting Ruth be sneaky and try to trick Boaz?

Do you think doing something wrong, even if for a good intention (to make sure Ruth is taken care of), is okay?

Boaz Responds

How did Boaz respond to Ruth's actions in verses 8-15?

What does this say about Boaz's character?

What does Boaz say about Ruth's character in v. 11?

What is in the way of Boaz marrying (redeeming) Ruth? (v. 12)

What do you think Ruth was feeling about hearing this news?

Boaz continues to protect Ruth and her reputation. He even sends her home with more grain.

All they can do now is wait and see what the reaction of the nearest potential guardian redeemer will say and do. But really, as with everything, it is in God's hands.

Small Group Discussion

Break into smaller groups to discuss the following:
- Discuss your thoughts on the story so far?
- What do you think will happen?
- What do you think about the character Ruth?

Spend some time talking about what you can do in your lives now and in the near future to demonstrate some of the positive character traits we have seen in Ruth (e.g. loyalty, hard work, obedience, etc.)

_____

_____

_____

_____

_____

Each group will have an opportunity to share some of the things they discussed with the big group.

How did the kindness shown by Boaz change the story?

Have you known anyone down and out like Naomi? How were you able to show them kindness and change their story? Do you wish you had done more or done things differently?

One way to show kindness is by serving others, which we will play a part in next week.

Why do you think it is important to serve others?

Sole Hope Shoe Cutting Party

Next week during our time together we will be doing a service project together for an organization called Sole Hope. They are located in Uganda in Africa. They clean and treat feet, as well as sew and provide shoes. Not only do they help the people with the shoes they provide, they also provide jobs for people there who make the shoes so they can take care of their families.

If you want to host your own Sole Hope shoe cutting party, you can purchase a kit at www.solehopeparty.org.

Week 3 Homework

- Reread Ruth chapter3 and the things we discussed about the chapter.
- Think more about your belief and confidence in our memory verse – that God can work all things for the good of those who love him, who have been called according to his purposes. Think about what it means to be called according to his purposes.
- Think more about your service project.
- Memorize Romans 8:28.

Make sure to **bring your items next week** for the service project. We need:
- Old jeans
- Fabric
- Good, sharp scissors
- Empty, rinsed out gallon milk (plastic)

Week 4: The Redeemer, Our Redeemer

Warm Up with tea and treats
- Place all of your items for the service project in the designated spaces.
- Make a card for one of the kids that will get the shoes you are making parts for today.

Memory Verse
- Take volunteers to recite the memory verse and get their prize.

Question Box
- Have the girls take turns answering a questions from the box.

Open in Prayer to start the study

Recap of Week 3
- Pick a volunteer to review week 3 discussion
- Review homework
- Discuss service project ideas

Read Ruth Chapter 4
- Listed on the following pages 30-32

Boaz Settles the Matter

4:1 Now Boaz went up to the village gate and sat there. Then along came the guardian whom Boaz had mentioned to Ruth! Boaz said, "Come here and sit down, 'John Doe'!" So he came and sat down. ² Boaz chose ten of the village leaders and said, "Sit down here!" So they sat down. ³ Then Boaz said to the guardian, "Naomi, who has returned from the region of Moab, is selling the portion of land that belongs to our relative Elimelech. ⁴ So I am legally informing you: Acquire it before those sitting here and before the leaders of my people! If you want to exercise your right to redeem it, then do so. But if not, then tell me so I will know. For you possess the first option to redeem it; I am next in line after you." He replied, "I will redeem it." ⁵ Then Boaz said, "When you acquire the field from Naomi, you must also acquire Ruth the Moabite, the wife of our deceased relative, in order to preserve his family name by raising up a descendant who will inherit his property." ⁶ The guardian said, "Then I am unable to redeem it, for I would ruin my own inheritance in that case. You may exercise my redemption option, for I am unable to redeem it." ⁷ (Now this used to be the customary way to finalize a transaction involving redemption in Israel: A man would remove his sandal and give it to the other party. This was a legally binding act in Israel.) ⁸ So the guardian said to Boaz, "You may acquire it," and he removed his sandal.

⁹ Then Boaz said to the leaders and all the people, "You are witnesses today that I have acquired from Naomi all that belonged to Elimelech, Kilion, and Mahlon. ¹⁰ I have also acquired Ruth the Moabite, the wife of Mahlon, as my wife to raise up a descendant who will inherit his property so the name of the deceased might not disappear from among his relatives and from his village. You are witnesses today." ¹¹ All the people who were at the gate and the elders replied, "We are witnesses. May the LORD make the woman who is entering your home like Rachel and Leah, both of whom built up the house of Israel! May you prosper in Ephrathah and become famous in Bethlehem. ¹² May your family become like the family of Perez—whom Tamar bore to Judah—through the descendants the LORD gives you by this young woman."

A Grandson is Born to Naomi

¹³ So Boaz married Ruth and had elations with her. The LORD enabled her to conceive and she gave birth to a son. ¹⁴ The village women said to Naomi, "May the LORD be praised because he has not left you without a guardian today! May he become famous in Israel! ¹⁵ He will encourage you and provide for you when you are old, for your daughter-in-law, who loves you, has given him birth. She is better to you than seven sons!" ¹⁶ Naomi took the child and placed him on her lap; she became his caregiver. ¹⁷ The neighbor women named him, saying, "A son has been born to Naomi." They named him Obed. Now he became the father of Jesse—David's father!

Epilogue: Obed in the Genealogy of David

[18] These are the descendants of Perez:
Perez was the father of Hezron,
[19] Hezron was the father of Ram,
Ram was the father of Amminadab,
[20] Amminadab was the father of Nachshon, Nachshon was the father of Salmah, [21] Salmon was the father of Boaz, Boaz was the father of Obed,
[22] Obed was the father of Jesse, and Jesse was the father of David.

Abraham was the father of Isaac, and Isaac the father of Jacob, and Jacob the father of Judah and his brothers, and Judah the father of Perez and Zerah by Tamar, and Perez the father of Hezron, and Hezron the father of Ram, and Ram the father of Amminadab, and Amminadab the father of Nahshon, and Nahshon the father of Salmon, and Salmon the father of Boaz by Rahab, and Boaz the father of Obed by Ruth, and Obed the father of Jesse, and Jesse the father of David the king. And David was the father of Solomon by the wife of Uriah, and Solomon the father of Rehoboam, and Rehoboam the father of Abijah, and Abijah the father of Asaph, and Asaph the father of Jehoshaphat, and Jehoshaphat the father of Joram, and Joram the father of Uzziah, and Uzziah the father of Jotham, and Jotham the father of Ahaz, and Ahaz the father of Hezekiah, and Hezekiah the father of Manasseh, and Manasseh the father of Amos, and Amos the father of Josiah, and Josiah the father of Jechoniah and his brothers, at the time of the deportation to Babylon. And after the deportation to Babylon: Jechoniah was the father of Shealtiel, and Shealtiel the father of Zerubbabel, and Zerubbabel the father of Abiud, and Abiud the father of Eliakim, and Eliakim the father of Azor, and Azor the father of Zadok, and Zadok the father of Achim, and Achim the father of Eliud, and Eliud the father of Eleazar, and Eleazar the father of Matthan, and Matthan the father of Jacob, and Jacob the father of Joseph the husband of Mary, of whom was born

JESUS
who is called Christ.

Who will redeem?

How many elders did Boaz select to serve as witnesses? (V.2)

In these times, the town gates were important centers of the city. Matters of commerce and issues were discussed and legal and business transactions were made.

The name of the kinsman with the first right of redemption is not given.

In addition to redeeming Ruth & Naomi what else needs to be redeemed? (v. 3)

The ancestral lands could never be permanently sold – only temporarily sold until the 50th year Jubilee when the land is given back to the original owner.

At first he is interested in being the kinsman redeemer, until he learns what? (v. 5)

Why was he not willing to be the redeemer? (v. 6)

How does Boaz finalize the transaction? (V. 7-8)

How did the village women praise Ruth?(v. 14-15)

What virtues do both Ruth and Boaz display?

How many names are in the genealogy in v. 18-22?

What other instances of the number 10 do we see?

- 10 years in Moab (1:4)
- Ten elders as witnesses (4:2)
- Ten name genealogy (4:18-22)

Ten is a number that symbolizes divine order.

What did you think about the end of the story?

Ruth's decision to remain loyal to Naomi started the lineage of Jesus, through King David. It is an extraordinary display of God's working all things for good.

What do you think about the fact that Boaz was the redeemer in this story, but ultimately was part of the family line of all of our redeemer – Jesus?

Does this change how you look at what Jesus did for you and me?

What does this story tell us about God's responsibility and our responsibility in working out God's plans?

Group Service Project: Sole Hope Shoe Cutting party

SOLE HOPE

1. Collect up your old jeans.
2. Cut out the patterns provided by Sole Hope*.
3. Trace the pattern onto the jeans and cut.

The cut jeans will be sent to Uganda where women & men, employed by Sole Hope, will craft them into shoes.

*If you want to host your own Sole Hope shoe cutting party, you can purchase a kit at www.solehopeparty.org.

Thank you for joining us on this journey through Ruth. Our hope and prayer is that you will continue to dig into God's Word. That you would love nothing more than getting to know God and to make Him known to those God has placed in your life.

We pray that you will be leaders among your peers, to do the right thing even, and especially, when it is not the easy thing. God has gifted each of you uniquely and He can't wait to watch your life unfold for His purposes and glory. God bless you!

Sources used:
The Ruth Bible text all come from the New English Translation (NET) version.
Ruth & Esther: A Double-Edged Bible Study, Think LifeChange, NavPress 2013
Ruth & Esther, Shepherd's Notes, Holman Reference, B&H Publishing, 1998
Agape Bible Study – The Book of Ruth, www.agapebiblestudy.com/Ruth

Attachments

Ice Breaker Questions

Who would you like to be other than yourself?
Which superhero would you like to be, and why?
What kind of magical power would you like to possess?
Which food would you like to eat endlessly?
Which other name would you like to be called by if not your own?
Where would you like to live, in the ocean or on the moon?
If you had the chance to transport yourself, where would you go and why?
If you had to give up a favorite food, what would it be and why?
Who's your favorite comic strip character? Would you like to be him/her?
Which animal would you prefer to be and why?
Narrate one incident where you got into big trouble with your parents.
What are your favorite hobbies?
What are your pet peeves or interesting things about you that you dislike?
What do you love to do the most in the world?
What is the one food you'd hate to waste and can't let others waste too?
Do you like reading books? Which is your favorite of all time?
Which television program do you love watching and can't miss even in the worst situation?
What do you love about summer?
Who do you consider your hero?
Would you rather be really hairy or completely bald?
Would you rather eat healthy or exercise regularly?
Would you rather super strong or super fast?
Would you rather lose half your hair or lose half your hearing?
Would you rather have to sit all day or stand all day?
Would you rather be in your pajamas all day or in a suit all day?
Would you rather be the most popular kid in school or the smartest kid in school?
Would you rather give out bad advice or receive bad advice?
Would you rather never play or play but always lose?
Would you rather take an ice cold shower and be clean or not shower at all?

Service Project Group Idea

Sole Hole is located in Uganda in Africa. They clean and treat feet, as well as sew and provide shoes. Not only do they help the people with the shoes they provide, they also provide jobs for people there who make the shoes so they can take care of their families.

They have a kit for a shoe cutting party where groups can use their guides to cut materials that will be made into shoes. The kit also includes a video you can watch together as a group to learn more about the organization and the people in Uganda they support.

You can purchase a kit at www.solehopeparty.org and learn more about the organization at www.solehope.org.

Other Service Ideas

Lemonade and cookie stand – help the kids research an organization to donate money to and during your small group time make lemonade and cookies together to sell in the neighborhood. Donate all proceeds to the charity.

Letters – write/draw notes to mail to grandparents or friends letting them know you are thinking of them and think they are special. You can work on them together during your small group time.

Neighbor gifts – bake cookies or make a small craft and deliver them with a note to some of your neighbors (especially those you don't know so well). You can make the crafts or cookies together as a group.

Knitting Party – buy a knitting craft kit from Kids Knits (www.kidknits.org) and have a knitting craft party. The kits are a fundraiser for the communities in Rwanda and Chile that make the yarn and contain instructions, handspun yarn and all of the tools (needle, loom, hook, carrying bag, etc). They even have "me and my doll" hat kits.

Surprise gifts – leave $1 with a note on an aisle at the dollar store (they can even use their allowance), leave a bag of popcorn with a note on a RedBox, leave a little gift and note on the mailbox for your mailman, bake & decorate a batch of cookies for your child's school or church office workers. Each girl can bring a few $1 bills and you can make the note cards together as a group. You can even all take a road trip to deliver them together.

Other Service Ideas

Craft/game day – contact a local children's home and plan an afternoon of fun with crafts, a movie & popcorn, or kickball tournament.

Donation jar – get a mason jar and decorate it using sharpies, buttons, ribbon, bling and a chalk board label (from Target or a craft store) to collect change. The kids can start learning to tithe their allowance by putting it in the jar. You can dump it out from time to time to donate to a cause or the church collection plate. You can use chalk to write what you are saving for. Decorating the jars is a fun art project to do during your small group time.

Homeless bags – make blessing bags (non-perishable snacks, toiletries, note) to keep in the car to hand out to someone in need you see. You can also stuff the items in a new pair of warm socks. Each girl can get a different item to bring 10 of and you can pack them together during your small group, as well as make cards with Bible verses to include in each.

Games for shelters – collect gently used board games/cards and deliver them to homeless shelters that take in kids

Nursing homes – contact a local nursing home to ask about coming to sing to the residents (you can practice a few easy songs with the kids) or plan a game night to play bingo or board games with them. You can bring homemade cards and flowers to leave behind.

Made in the USA
Columbia, SC
17 April 2025